ABOVE: *Sheep shearing has changed little over the years; the machinery used today is similar to that developed in the late nineteenth century. This picture was taken at Witney in 1969, when the blanket firm of Charles Early and Marriott celebrated its three hundredth anniversary by setting up a new 'sheep to blanket' record. Four men began shearing at 4 a.m. The aim was to produce fifty pure wool blankets during the hours of daylight, including six within 10 hours 27 minutes, the old record. The six blankets were produced in 8 hours 11 minutes.*

FRONT COVER: *Cloth dressers in the cropping shop, from George Walker's 'The Costume of Yorkshire' (1814).*

THE WOOLLEN INDUSTRY

Chris Aspin

Shire Publications Ltd

CONTENTS

Printed in Great Britain by CIT Printing Services, Press Buildings, Merlins Bridge, Haverfordwest, Dyfed SA61 1XF.

Published in 1994 by Shire Publications Ltd, Cromwell House, Church Street, Princes Risborough, Buckinghamshire HP27 9AJ, UK. Copyright © 1982 by Chris Aspin. First published 1982; reprinted 1985, 1987, 1991 and 1994. Shire Album 81. ISBN 0 85263 598 2.

ACKNOWLEDGEMENTS
The author and publishers are grateful for the assistance in the preparation of this book of Mr J. C. S. Magson, Metropolitan Borough of Calderdale Museums and Art Galleries Service. Illustrations are acknowledged as follows: Bradford Industrial Museum, page 9 (top); British Wool Textile Industry Press Office, page 19 (bottom); Calderdale Museums Service, cover and pages 15 (bottom right), 16 (bottom), 31; Carpet Manufacturing Company, Kidderminster, page 24 (top); M. Davies-Shiel, page 29 (bottom); National Museum of Antiquities of Scotland, page 5; Scapa Group, page 26 (top); Scottish Tourist Board, page 24 (bottom); J. C. D. Smith, pages 3, 7 (right); Welsh Tourist Board, page 17; Whitbread's, page 27 (bottom left and right).

FURTHER READING
Davies-Shiel, M. *Wool Is My Bread.* (The Kendal woollen trade up to 1575.)
Heaton, H. *The Yorkshire Woollen and Worsted Industries.*
Jenkins, J. G. (editor). *The Wool Textile Industry of Great Britain.*
Jenkins, J. G. *The Welsh Woollen Industry.*
Lipson, E. *History of the English Woollen and Worsted Industries.*
Ponting, K. G. *The Woollen Industry of South-west England.*
Reach, A. B. *The Yorkshire Textile Districts in 1849.*

The Piece Hall, Halifax, was opened in 1779 as a market for the numerous 'small masters' producing cloth over a wide area. It was built on a slope with three storeys on the lower side and two on the higher. There were 315 rooms, taken by the clothiers. The weekly market was held on Saturday mornings. The cloth was bought by wholesale merchants and much of it was exported. There were similar halls in Leeds, Huddersfield, Bradford, Wakefield and Colne. The engraving is from 'The History of the Town and Parish of Halifax' by E. Jacobs (1789).

The church of St Peter and St Paul at Lavenham, the best preserved of the medieval 'wool' towns of Suffolk, owes its splendour to wool, like many other churches in East Anglia, the Cotswolds and the West Country. Much of the cost of rebuilding the church in the late fifteenth century was borne by Thomas Spring, a wealthy clothier.

INTRODUCTION

The wool textile industry occupies a unique place in British history. From the twelfth century to the nineteenth (when it was eclipsed by the upstart cotton trade) the woollen manufacture had no rival. As one writer put it in 1683, 'There are many more people employed and more profit made and money imported by the making of cloth than by all the other manufactories of England put together.' Forty years later Daniel Defoe described English woollen goods as 'the richest and most valuable manufacture in the world'. No other industry has enjoyed so great a prestige or

has been carried on in so many places for so long a time. In the words of a recent historian, 'There was probably not a town, village or hamlet throughout the length and breadth of the country which was not connected at some time or other with the manufacture of cloth. It was the universal character of the woollen industry which gave it its peculiar significance, since in its progress and development were bound up the national fortunes and the interests of every section of the community.' For hundreds of years the spinning wheel and the handloom were found in almost every home; the fulling mill was as common as the corn mill; and it was impossible to travel far without passing fields full of tenterframes, on which cloth was stretched and dried. All over Britain inn signs remind us of the once ubiquitous woollen trade. The Fleece, the Ram, the Woolpack and others occur again and again. Here and there one comes across less familiar signs such as the Bishop Blaize (the patron saint of woolcombers) and, equally puzzling to recent generations, the Bay and Say (names of cloths) and the Pandy (the Welsh for 'fulling mill').

The former importance of the industry is reflected in the numerous 'wool' churches, guildhalls, clothiers' and workers' houses, public buildings and factories. The English language has been greatly enriched by sayings and phrases that have come down to us from what were once everyday activities: 'spinning a yarn', 'on tenterhooks', 'dyed in the wool', 'a web of lies' and many more. Street and field names recall the old occupations, as do the surnames of many thousands of British people. Weaving has given us Weaver, Webster, Webber and Webb; fulling Fuller, Tucker and Walker; dyeing Dyer and Lister. There are many others. On every journey we make, in every group of people we meet and in every book or article we read, there will probably be reminders that the woollen industry was once all-powerful in Britain.

BELOW LEFT: *This monumental brass in the church at Chipping Norton, Oxfordshire, depicts John Yonge, a woolman who died in 1451. Note the woolpacks on which he stands.*

BELOW RIGHT: *Weaving in the early fifteenth century. The horizontal loom had then been in general use for about two centuries; in earlier looms the warp threads were fixed vertically on a wooden frame. The foot treadles of the horizontal loom enabled the weaver to raise and lower alternate selections of warp threads and thus produce a patterned cloth by passing the shuttle through the 'shed' so formed. No major improvement was made to the handloom until John Kay patented his fly shuttle in 1733.*

The distaff and spindle have been used for spinning wool since prehistoric times. The method was universal until the introduction of the spinning wheel in the thirteenth century and continued in remote areas until the early 1800s. The girl holds the distaff under one arm and from the rovings wound around the forked top draws a continuous strand, which she attaches to the wooden spindle. To impart twist she spins the spindle with her finger and thumb. A 'whorl' keeps the spindle upright and acts as a flywheel. Each length of spun yarn is wound on to the spindle.

HISTORY OF THE WOOLLEN INDUSTRY

Woollen cloth has been made in Britain for several thousand years; no one knows when the first pieces were woven but, as excavations in Somerset have shown, there was a well developed industry in the lake villages of Glastonbury and Meare as long ago as the iron age. The Romans, who thought highly of British wool, expanded the manufacturing of goods to such an extent that by the third century hard-wearing rugs and capes were the country's principal exports. The Romans also built the first factory in Britain. This was a military weaving establishment (*gynaeceum*) set up by the Emperor Diocletian at Winchester. A dye works is believed to have existed at Silchester and there were cloth-finishing shops (*fullonicae*) in the major towns.

During the dark ages sheep came to be valued more for their ability to manure land for corn and other crops than for their wool and it was only after the Norman conquest that sheep breeding was seriously pursued. Industry was also expanded, but though guilds of weavers were established in London and other centres and though fine British cloths were exported throughout the twelfth and thirteenth centuries, the trade in wool remained much more important than its manufacture. The great landowning abbeys sold vast numbers of fleeces to Italy, Germany and the Low Countries, using much of the income to pay for the construction of their splendid buildings. The abbots frequently made long-term contracts with foreign buyers and on one occasion an Italian company agreed to buy the whole of the Kirkstall (Leeds) clip for ten years. Wool was often used instead of money, as in 1194 when English fleeces provided the ransom for

Richard the Lion Heart, who had been imprisoned in Austria while returning from a Crusade.

Despite the great profits that came from wool during the thirteenth and early fourteenth centuries, a feeling grew that England should make more of its own goods. The woollen industry was in decline and its revival depended on an injection of new skills. This began in the 1330s when Edward III chose a time of unrest in the Low Countries to invite Flemish weavers, fullers and dyers to settle in England under his protection. Their arrival revitalised the decaying industry and, in the words of one historian, 'revealed to England her true destiny and helped to prepare the day for her transformation from a land of agricultural labourers into a land of industrial artisans'. In the middle years of the fourteenth century, England exported about five thousand pieces of cloth annually; within two hundred years the number was twenty times greater. Wool growing replaced corn growing in order to meet the demand of the busy looms, the cloth from which found its way through companies of Merchant Adventurers to every known market in the world.

This early industrial revolution had far reaching consequences. The raw wool trade came under the control of merchants – the *broggers* and *staplers* – and at the same time capitalist employers – the *clothiers* – challenged the old guild system by organising the manufacture and distribution of cloth. Some of the merchants and clothiers became rich enough to build the magnificent 'wool' churches of the Cotswolds, East Anglia and the West Country; their northern and Welsh counterparts usually operated on a much more modest scale. Foreign workers continued to come to Britain, and of particular importance was the arrival of Dutch and Walloon weavers seeking religious freedom in the sixteenth century. Their ability to produce a wide range of attractive 'new draperies' from combed wool (worsteds) did much to restore the fortunes of Norwich, which had four thousand aliens by 1572, Colchester and other towns.

As the woollen trade expanded, the power of the guilds weakened further. Despite their commendable concern for equality and high standards of workmanship, they had become choked by a mass of rules, the interpretation of which led frequently to demarcation and other disputes. To gain its freedom, the industry moved away from the guild-dominated towns and into rural areas, where fulling mills were more easily established. In Yorkshire, for instance, the old manufacturing centres of York and Beverley declined at the expense of the West Riding, which can trace its origin as a large-scale supplier of cloth to this sixteenth century migration. As competition took the place of medieval regulations, the guilds gradually gave way to a domestic system of manufacture and even to a few factories. The best remembered of these was that built in the sixteenth century by John Winchcombe (Jack of Newbury). Thomas Deloney described it in verse:

'Within one room being large and long
There stood two hundred Looms full strong:
Two hundred men the truth is so
Wrought in these Looms all in a row.'

Though Deloney may have been exaggerating – he goes on to list large numbers of other workers – there is no doubt that Winchcombe was a true factory master. There were others like him, notably William Stumpe, who filled Malmesbury and Osney abbeys with his looms, and a Burford clothier named Tuckar, who undertook a similar venture at Abingdon. Generally, however, the clothiers employed people who worked in their own homes; the domestic system, despite its inefficiencies, was not finally extinguished until the nineteenth century.

As Britain's principal source of wealth, the woollen industry enjoyed many privileges. 'The government', said one writer, 'lavished upon it the most unremitting care and attention and created for its protection an elaborate code of industrial and commercial regulations'. By the end of the eighteenth century, there were more than three hundred laws covering everything from the clipping of sheep to the length, breadth, weight and 'true making' of cloth. The most important piece of legislation was the proclamation of James I prohibiting the export of wool, a policy which lasted until 1824. Its aim was to ensure that

PANNUS·MIHI·PANIS

KENDAL

ABOVE: *The woolhooks and teasels (used for raising a nap on cloth) on the arms of Kendal and the motto 'Wool is my bread' indicate the town's former dependence on the woollen trade. The earliest record of the arms is on a tankard of 1629. Civic heraldry includes many references to wool: Boston, Guildford, Godalming, Pudsey, Rawtenstall, Rochdale and Wolverhampton have coats depicting woolpacks; a fleece appears in the arms of Bacup, Bury, Leeds and Nelson; rams or ram's heads were chosen by Bradford, Boston, Godalming, Leominster and Westmorland.*

RIGHT: *A sixteenth-century cloth finisher and the tools he used are carved on this wooden bench-end in Spaxton church, Somerset. The workman appears to be brushing cloth or pressing it with a hot iron to give it a satiny lustre. In both pieces of cloth are the holes made by tenterhooks. To the left of the upper piece is a teasel frame and to the right a comb. The workman is flanked by hand shears and a burling knife used to remove knots left in the cloth by the weaver. A bench-end in East Budleigh church, Devon, shows hand shears and a frame filled with teasels.*

manufacturers had an abundant supply of raw material at low prices, but so great was the demand for English wool abroad that it gave rise to smuggling on a vast scale. The escapades involving the 'owlers' and the government officers who tried to arrest them provide some of the most exciting incidents of English history. William Carter, who spent much of his life in pursuit of the owlers, was several times pursued himself. On Romney Marsh in 1688 he and his companions were chased by fifty armed horsemen; on another occasion, when Carter arrested a smuggler at Folkestone, 'the women of the town came out of their houses and gathered up stones on the beach, which they flung about my ears so violently that I was forced to quit my prisoner, hardly escaping myself'.

After the Civil War the capitalist classes, which secured control of Parliament, removed the restraints on the woollen industry, leaving employer and employed to determine conditions of work. Trade

A report from the Leeds Mercury of the murder in April 1812 of William Horsfall, a manufacturer hated by the Luddites for his introduction of machinery. One of the murderers confessed to his part in the crime to save his life. His three companions were hanged.

unions, or combinations as they were then called, became a feature of English life, often growing out of clubs set up to help members in times of distress. Weavers and woolcombers were among the first groups to clash with their masters. After riots during the early eighteenth century, Parliament in 1726 outlawed combinations formed with the aim of regulating industry and improving conditions of labour. After only a few more years, serious riots occurred in the West Country and Wiltshire, where three men were hanged for destroying a clothier's house and property. Much more serious were the Luddite outrages in Nottinghamshire and West Yorkshire between 1811 and 1816. The framework knitters, angered by a fall in living standards, destroyed frames owned by masters who cut wages. The Yorkshiremen saw new machinery, in particular the cropping frame and the gig mill, as a threat to their livelihood. They murdered one millowner, fired on another and attacked mills. Fourteen Luddites were hanged at York and six at Nottingham.

Not until the factory system swept away domestic production were the combinations enfeebled or destroyed. It was only in the twentieth century that organised labour in the woollen trade became a strong force again.

The revolutionary textile inventions of the eighteenth and nineteenth centuries enabled woollen and worsted goods to be mass-produced in power-driven factories, though the changeover from the domestic system took longer to complete than in the cotton districts. There were two basic reasons for this. First, cotton was much cheaper and more plentiful than wool; American supplies of cotton were available long before the wool-growing industries of Australia, South Africa and New Zealand made their impact. Secondly, power-loom weaving of woollen cloth and the combing of worsted by machinery presented technical difficulties which were not overcome until the middle of the nineteenth century. One development caused by the scarcity of wool was the birth and rapid expansion of the *shoddy* trade, which made cheap cloth by reworking ground-up rags from both Britain and abroad. Dewsbury became the centre of the trade, which began in Batley in about 1813. The low cost of cotton prompted manufacturers to experiment with cotton warps to produce *mixed* goods which were both cheap and attractively designed. By 1830 the new lines were immensely popular and in 1858 it was estimated that ninety-five per cent of worsteds were mixed with cotton, which made up a third of their weight.

The industrial revolution, as one writer put it, 'had the most remarkable effects upon the geographical distribution of the woollen and worsted industries. Instead of being carried on in every part of the country, in innumerable towns, villages and hamlets, they were now concentrated mainly in the West Riding of Yorkshire.' Even before the great inventions, the West Riding had achieved a position of pre-eminence. Its rate of progress quickened throughout the eighteenth century until by 1770 it had overtaken the Norwich area as a producer of worsteds and was responsible for more than half of Britain's entire export trade in fabrics. The population of the West Riding increased from 572,000 in 1801 to 1,325,000 half a century later; old towns like Halifax and Leeds were vastly expanded and new towns like Huddersfield were created out of mere hamlets in less than half a century. Life in these crowded and insanitary places was often unspeakably bad. The journalist Angus

ABOVE: *A girl tending a spinning frame at a Yorkshire mill in 1900.*

BELOW: *A view of Leeds from 'The Graphic' of 1885. Mills and workers' houses were crowded together beneath the smoke from innumerable chimneys, as the industry expanded rapidly.*

9

ABOVE LEFT: *Before the woollen industry moved from the home into the factory, it passed through a brief intermediate stage in which production was carried out in workshops like this one at Rawtenstall, Lancashire, which dates from the late eighteenth century, when spinning and weaving were still hand processes. Note the 'triplet' windows, installed to give the workers the maximum light. The building has been restored by Rawtenstall Civic Society.*

ABOVE RIGHT: *Children leaving a Yorkshire mill in 1814. Until steam engines came into general use, water was the main source of power and the early mills were often far from the main centres of population. In front of the mill are seams of tenters on which cloth has been hooked to dry. From George Walker's 'The Costume of Yorkshire' (1814).*

BELOW: *Strict rules governed the lives of mill workers and disobedience brought stiff fines, as can be seen from this entry in a wage book of 1851, from a Helmshore mill. To arrive at work unshaven cost 6d and offences relating to drink as much as 5s, a third of a week's pay.*

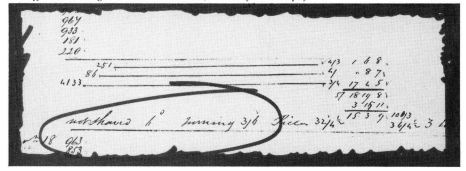

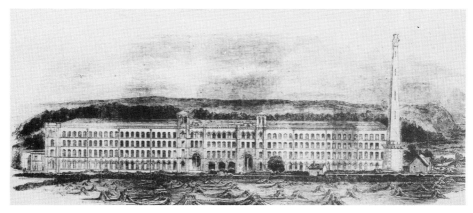

'We have built a palace of industry to equal the palaces of the Caesars', said the Mayor of Bradford at the opening in 1853 of Saltaire Mill. Sir Titus Salt was the first man to spin alpaca hair successfully, thus founding an important new branch of the woollen industry. Alpaca had been brought from South America in the early 1800s, but had proved too difficult to work until Salt began experimenting in 1836. From his immense profits he built, during the course of twenty years, the mill, eight hundred houses, a church, public baths and wash-houses, almshouses, an infirmary, an institute and a park. The mill is as long as St Paul's Cathedral (545 feet or 166 metres) and the chimney is 250 feet (76 metres) high. When the mill was opened, five steam engines drove 3 miles (4800 metres) of shafting. Every effort was made to provide good lighting, warmth and ventilation.

Reach said of Leeds in 1849: 'The condition of vast districts of the town is such as the very strongest language cannot overstate . . . Conceive acre on acre of closely built and thickly peopled ground, without a paving stone upon the surface or an inch of sewer beneath, a deep trodden-churned slough of mud forming the only thoroughfares . . . Conceive streets and courts and yards which a scavenger never appears to have entered since King John incorporated Leeds and which give the idea of a town built in a slimy bog . . . Conceive, in short, a whole district to which the above description rigidly and truthfully applies and you will, I am sorry to say, have a fair idea of what constitutes a large proportion of the operative part of Leeds.'

Conditions in the first factories were equally uncomfortable, for as well as the long hours, low wages and bad working conditions which were carried over from the domestic system there was the strict discipline of a routine dictated by the untiring steam engine. The ill treatment of young children aroused widespread indignation and led to the founding of the Factory Movement, which after a long struggle persuaded Parliament to limit the number of hours worked and to set up a paid factory inspectorate. State interference on behalf of the working classes was an important departure from the widely held view that manufacturers should have a completely free hand in dealing with labour and in the internal running of their mills.

Working conditions varied tremendously, as Angus Reach found in 1849. During a short visit to the West Riding, he was able to contrast the lives of the domestic workers of Saddleworth with those of the mill operatives in the big towns. Of the moorland farmer-weavers he wrote: 'High up on the hillside above Delph I counted from one point of view a couple of dozen cottages, in each of which the loom was going, and around each of which the kine were grazing. It was a glorious sunny afternoon, and amid the fields and by the roadside, the weavers with their wives and children were many of them stretching out their warps upon a rude apparatus of sticks to dry them in the genial air. The gay tinting of many of these outstretched meshes of thread, glancing along the green of hedges or the cold grey of stone walls, made quite a feature of the landscape.' In one cottage 'in which dirty beds lay unmade in the workshop', the weaver told Reach that work was uncertain and 'spoke bitterly of the power loom, which would, he was afraid, in the long run beat him and his comrades out of the field. He lived upon potatoes, porridge, oatcake and milk, and meat "when he could catch it".'

At a shoddy mill in Dewsbury, Reach found a very different scene. 'The establishment is devoted solely to the sorting, preparing and grinding of rags, which are worked up in the neighbouring factories. Great bales choke full of filthy tatters lay scattered about the yard, and loaded wagons were fast arriving and adding to the heap. As for the mill, a glance at its exterior showed its character. It being a calm, still day, the walls and part of the roof were covered with thick clinging dust and fibre, which ascended in choky volumes from the open doors and glassless windows of the ground floor, and which also poured forth from a chimney, constructed for the purpose, exactly like smoke. I was told that on a windy day the appearance of the place would be by no means so bad, as a through draught would carry the dust rapidly away to leeward. As it was, however, the mill was covered as with a mildewy fungus, and upon the grey slates of the roof the frowzy deposit could not be less than two inches in depth.' In the room where the rags were torn to pieces by the revolving teeth of machines called 'devils', Reach watched the choking dust burst out from door and window and 'it was not until a minute or so that I could see the workmen. On the floor, the dust and coarse filaments lay as if, to use the quaint phrase of a gentleman present, "it had been snowing snuff". The workmen were, of course, coated with the flying powder. They wore bandages over their mouths so as to prevent as much as possible the inhalation of the dust, and seemed loath to remove the protection for a moment.'

At a Batley shoddy mill, Reach found 'a perfect whirlwind of pungent titillating powder'. The operatives were Irishwomen, who 'with their squalid, dust-strewn garments, powdered to a dull greyish hue, and with their bandages tied over the greater part of their faces, moved like reanimated mummies in their swathings; I had seldom seen anything more ghastly.'

The Yorkshire factory reformers, who established Short-Time Committees to organise demonstrations and to get up petitions throughout the textile districts, were drawn from many walks of life but were mostly Tory or Radical in politics and Anglican or Primitive Methodist in religion. Their leader was Richard Oastler, a ceaseless campaigner who was idolised as the 'Factory King'. One of his first recruits was a Bingley landowner and Tory MP, William Busfeild Ferrand, whose attacks on the mill masters earned him the title of the 'Working Man's Friend'. Here is Ferrand's own account of his conversion to the cause he so vigorously supported: 'At the hour of five on a winter's morning, I left my home to shoot wild fowl. On my road, I had to pass along a deep and narrow lane which led from a rural village to a distant factory. The wind howled furiously; the snow fell heavily and drifted before the bitter blast. I indistinctly traced three children's footsteps. Soon, I heard a piteous cry of distress. Hurrying on, again I listened, but all was silent except the distant tolling of the factory bell. Again I tracked their footmarks and saw that one had lagged behind; I returned and found the little factory slave half-buried in a snowdrift fast asleep. I dragged it from its winding sheet; the icy hand of death had congealed its blood and paralysed its limbs. In a few minutes it would have been "where the wicked cease from troubling and the weary are at rest". I aroused it from its stupor and saved its life. From that hour I became a "Ten Hours' Bill Man" and the unflinching advocate of "protection to native industry".'

During the twenty-five years after 1850 the wool textile trade experienced its most rapid expansion, though its importance in the national economy declined as new industries grew up. The greatest stimulus came from the 'ready-made' clothing makers, who were quick to adopt the sewing machine (invented in 1851) and the woodworkers' bandsaw, which was ideal for cutting layers of cloth. The first sewing machines were operated either by hand or

ABOVE: *For more than a century, Manningham Mills, Bradford, produced worsted and silk goods; and though they are no longer used for manufacturing, they are an impressive reminder of Yorkshire's former textile greatness. Samuel Cunliffe Lister (later Lord Masham) built the mills in 1873 from the fortunes he made from numerous inventions. The floor space is 26 acres (10.5 ha) and the chimney, built in the style of an Italian bell tower and known as Lister's Pride, is 255 feet (78 metres) high.*

RIGHT: *Pryce Jones's mill at Welshpool. Jones was the pioneer of mail order and supplied many of the crowned heads of Europe. The picture comes from one of his catalogues: note the leeks and the amusing verse.*

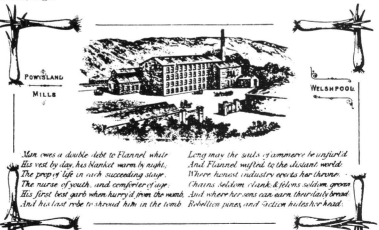

POWYSLAND MILLS

WELSHPOOL

Man owes a double debt to Flannel while
His vest by day, his blanket warm by night;
The prop of life in each succeeding stage,
The nurse of youth, and comforter of age:
His first best garb when hurry'd from the womb,
And his last robe to shroud him in the tomb.

Long may the sails of commerce be unfurl'd
And Flannel wafted to the distant world.
Where honest industry erects her throne,
Chains seldom clank & felons seldom groan
And where her sons can earn their daily bread,
Rebellion pines, and faction hides her head.

13

by treadle, but as early as 1854 George Holloway and Company of Stroud were using steam. 'Sewing by steam' enabled each operative to produce 150 pairs of men's trousers a week.

In Newtown, Wales, there began in 1859 a venture which was to be widely copied in succeeding years. This was the mail order business in flannels started by Pryce Jones, whose marketing techniques were well ahead of his time. From his small shop he sent out patterns to the local gentry and met with such a good response that in less than twenty years he claimed to have more than a hundred thousand patrons in all parts of the world. The London and North Western Railway Company built special vans to carry Jones's parcels and ran a daily service to Euston. Newtown was dubbed 'the Leeds of Wales', but its prosperity was not to last. The Montgomery-shire woollen industry declined and Jones had to look to Rochdale for his supplies.

The twentieth century has seen immense changes in the wool textile industry, which has been affected by the growth of manufacturing in other countries, by changes in fashion and by the introduction of man-made fibres. Though the size of the industry has been greatly diminished – 50,000 workers in 1980, compared with 275,000 in 1890 – the quality of its products has been steadily improved. Competition from abroad brought home to British firms the value of science as a means of survival. Universities, colleges and research centres have achieved notable successes both in the development of new machinery and in giving wool greater versatility by changing its natural properties. We are all familiar with garments which can be washed easily and which have an in-built range of 'easy-care' characteristics.

Government protection in 1932 marked the end of free trade: a twenty per cent duty on incoming fabrics and a ten per cent duty on incoming yarns did little to stem the industry's decline however, and more than thirty thousand workers left in the years preceding the Second World War. The trend towards larger groupings after 1950 was another response to contracting demand, but by this time wool textiles accounted for less than two per cent of the gross national product. Despite its many problems, today's slimmed-down industry is an important exporter, with customers in more than 170 countries. The reputation of British woollens and worsteds has never been higher.

Sorting wool in a Lancashire mill. The sorter's task is to grade the wool in the fleece, putting lengths of similar quality in the skips by his table. A good fleece will have as many as twelve different types of wool, the best being from around the shoulders and the next best from the back. The sorter notes the length and strength of the fibres, their softness and colour. The middle part of the table is composed of slats, through which dust and impurities fall.

ABOVE: *Bishop Blaize, depicted on a late eighteenth-century trade token from Exeter, was the patron saint of wool-combers and bishop of Sebaste in Asia Minor in the fourth century. Legend attributes the invention of the wool comb to him and he is said to have been tortured with his own device. The festival of St Blaize falls on 3rd February, when cele-brations were formerly held by wool-combers.*

TOP AND RIGHT: *The combing of wool to produce a long smooth yarn was the last major process to be mechanised. The early fourteenth-century illustrations (top) show combing to have been a woman's task; later it was undertaken by men, who spent long hours wielding heavy combs in workshops filled with the fumes from the charcoal-fuelled pots in which they heated the steel teeth of their implements. The photograph shows a reconstructed combing shop of the late eighteenth century. The woolcomber used two combs, each with several rows of teeth. One comb was fixed to a post and the other was swung against it. He then drew the fibres into a long sliver, passing it through a horn disc to keep the diameter uniform. About twenty slivers were formed into a 'top', one of which can be seen in the basket.*

LEFT: *Crank Mill, built in 1790 at Morley, was one of the first steam-driven mills in Yorkshire. It attracted many sightseers because part of the beam, the connecting rod, the crank and the flywheel were outside the building. The mill prepared wool for spinning.*

BELOW: *An early nineteenth-century spinning jenny, used at Saddleworth until 1916. The jenny patented by James Hargreaves in 1770 was too small to spin wool, but the improved and larger version was quickly adopted in the woollen districts, where it was worked long after it had become obsolete in the cotton trade. Power was never applied to the jenny, which enjoyed its greatest popularity when the industry was moving out of the home and into small workshops and factories. The Saddleworth jenny is now in the Piece Hall Museum, Halifax.*

A spinning mule at Brynkir Mills in Wales. The machine was widely used in the woollen trade, but is now almost obsolete.

HOW CLOTH IS MADE

The British wool textile industry draws its raw materials from many sources to produce a wide range of products – cloths of many varieties, furnishing fabrics, knitwear, blankets, carpets and felt. While raw wool is the principal material used, the industry makes substantial quantities of fabric from reworked waste. Cashmere, mohair, camel and other natural fibres, either alone or blended, also have their place, as do man-made fibres, which give strength and decoration when mixed with wool. The industry has three main sections: the fine woollen trade, which uses short-staple fibres; the low woollen trade, which uses waste; and the worsted trade, which depends mainly on the longer-staple fibres. Woollen cloth is woven from yarns in which the fibres are intermingled and lie in all directions; worsted cloth is woven from yarns spun from wool which has been combed to lay the fibres parallel. Woollen goods have a fluffy surface; those of worsted are smooth. Felt is a non-woven material made by compression, heat and moisture. The industry is now concentrated in Yorkshire, but there are important centres in Scotland, the West Country, Lancashire, Northern Ireland and Wales.

To transform a fleece into a finished article requires many processes, which are described briefly on the following pages.

SORTING AND SCOURING

After wool has been delivered to a mill, it is carefully sorted, each fleece being divided by hand into its numerous qualities. Scouring removes dirt, natural grease and other impurities, which can account for half the weight of the wool. By-products obtained at this stage include lanolin, which is used in cosmetics, soaps, ointments and polishes. Scouring was formerly carried out in fulling mills. Cloth was immersed in stale urine (*lant*) or covered with hog's dung and then beaten in the stocks. Today wool is passed through a series of wash bowls containing a detergent. Vegetable matter not washed away during scouring is removed by an acid treatment known as carbonising.

The woollen and worsted industries at this point go their separate ways. Let us consider first the subsequent processes in the woollen mill.

BLENDING

This is a vital step in which wools of different qualities and colours are mixed together.

CARDING

The carding engine, the largest machine in the industry, consists of a series of large and small cylinders covered with closely set wire teeth. As the blended wool passes through the machine, the revolving cylinders tease it out into a fine web of intermingled fibres. On leaving the carding engine, the web is *condensed* – divided into loose threads called slivers. Carding was originally done by working the wool between two hand-held boards set with wires. Automation was pioneered in the cotton industry, for which Richard Arkwright built a series of preparation machines, including the first continuous carding engine. His ideas were quickly adopted by woollen manufacturers.

PREPARATION OF WORSTED YARN

After scouring, worsted material is straightened out, washed and dried before passing to the combing machine. This is the heart of the worsted manufacture and its purpose is to remove the short fibres and allow the long ones to go forward. The short fibres, or *noils,* are an important raw material of the woollen trade. The combed sliver containing the long fibres is wound into a ball called a *top* ready for drawing and spinning. Combing was the last of the old hand processes to be mechanised. The Reverend Edmund Cartwright, inventor of the power loom, patented the first machine comb in 1790, following it two years later with another. Cartwright tried to copy the actions of the hand comber and his second machine became known as Big Ben because its action resembled the gestures of a prizefighter of that name. Though Big Ben was not a great success, it incorporated ideas developed by other inventors. The best known of these – Heilmann, Lister, Donisthorpe, Noble and Holden – patented machines between 1846 and 1856, by which time hand combing was almost extinct. In recent years worsted-type yarns have been produced by the so-called *semi-worsted system,* which uses carding, gilling and spinning, but no combing.

SPINNING

To produce a thread firm enough for weaving, loose slivers are drawn out and twisted. Spinning mills produce many kinds of yarn in several forms: large beams of warps, small pirns of weft for the shuttle, cones for knitting machines, hanks for the hand knitter. At the start of the eighteenth century all yarns were spun on single-thread devices – spinning wheels or the ancient distaff and spindle. By the end of the century power-driven machinery was widely used. Again it was the cotton industry which gave the lead, with the inventions of Hargreaves (the spinning jenny), Arkwright (the water frame) and Crompton (the mule). Ring frames, an improvement on Arkwright's basic design, are the most commonly used machines today. New ideas have not been lacking, however, and several systems have been developed in recent years. The aim of the designers has been to overcome the limitation under which spinning processes have previously worked – the need to rotate the yarn package in order to produce twist. *Break* or *open-end* machines, by introducing a gap in the flow of fibres, overcome this drawback and by doing so enable large packages to be made in a form suitable for the next process. New methods of

RIGHT: *Cartwright's 'Big Ben', the combing machine of 1792. Point X can be regarded as the 'shoulder' and B the 'arm' of what was called the 'crank lasher'. A was the principal comb, circular and with its teeth pointing inwards. D was a 'clearing' comb, which produced a fringe of fibres from tufts fed to the circular comb by the lasher. The fringe was drawn off by the two pairs of rollers (E) and was passed to the 'conducting' rollers (F), from which came a sliver.*

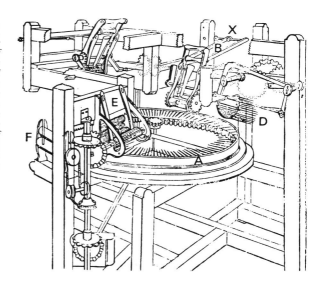

BELOW: *A Noble combing machine. During this process the comb extracts the short fibres (known as 'noils') and lays the longer fibres in a parallel formation to form a 'top', which is the basic material for the production of worsted yarn. This operation takes place after the grease and vegetable matter have been removed from the wool.*

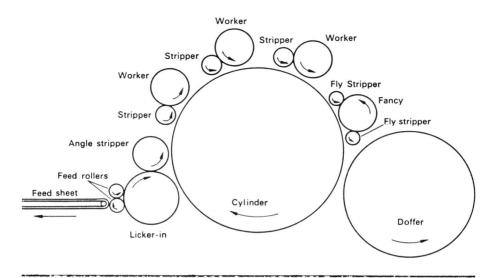

Worker

Stripper   Worker

Stripper

Worker

Fly Stripper

Stripper   Fancy

Fly stripper

Angle stripper

Feed rollers

Feed sheet

Cylinder

Doffer

Licker-in

Ground level

ABOVE: *A section of a modern woollen carding engine, showing the basic parts. The cylinder is 50 inches (1270 mm) in diameter. The woollen card was developed from the cotton card but has grown more complicated, being used for both the opening and mixing of fibres. This is achieved by placing pairs of 'worker' and 'stripper' rollers around the cylinder. The doffer removes the fibres, which are then passed on to another cylinder.*

BELOW: *Part of a woollen carding engine made by William Tatham, of Rochdale. It has a delivery speed of 40 yards (37 metres) a minute. Carding engines are the most complicated textile machines. A typical machine has eighty rollers and is more than 75 feet (23 metres) long. The main purpose of the carding engine is to reduce an entangled mass of fibres to a filmy web.*

20

Power-loom weaving of worsted at Ackroyd's mill, Halifax, in 1843. Patterns were held in sets of punched cards suspended above the looms. In this weaving shed there were 816 looms (seventeen rows with 48 looms in each).

spinning are still being developed and faster spindle speeds are being achieved.

WEAVING

Anyone who has darned a sock will understand the basic principle of weaving. A number of threads are first sewn in one direction; then, at right angles, more threads are passed over and under the first group to form a simple piece of fabric. This is what happens in a loom. One set of threads, which unwinds from a beam, makes up the *warp;* the crossways threads, which are delivered by a shuttle or some other device, are the *weft.* Variations in the 'over and under' passage of the weft give different surfaces to the cloth. Stripes and patterns can be introduced by using coloured threads. More complicated designs are held in punched (Jacquard) cards, which 'instruct' the loom to raise different combinations of warp threads before each insertion of weft. Old weaving

methods persisted for centuries. The most notable improvement to the medieval loom was the fly shuttle patented by John Kay in 1733. By flicking a cord to jerk a wheeled shuttle across the loom, the weaver was able to insert weft rapidly into wide fabric. The invention was adopted slowly by the tradition-bound industry and as late as 1822 there were riots at Frome when manufacturers introduced it. Power-loom weaving took more than half a century to perfect, many inventors following in the footsteps of Edmund Cartwright, who took out his first patent in 1785. By 1850 most worsted weaving was by power, but there were still handlooms at work in the woollen trade thirty years later. This was because woollen yarn, which has to be loosely spun, broke easily in the cumbersome first generation of power looms. Modern technology has transformed weaving dramatically and looms have been developed in which weft is rapidly inserted

21

ABOVE LEFT: *A stocking knitter at work in 1800. He is using a machine invented in 1589 by the Reverend William Lee, curate of Calverton, Nottinghamshire. Lee and his brother experimented with various methods of interlocking loops of woollen thread to form a knitted fabric, which could be folded and seamed to form a stocking. Framework knitting was a complicated process using a large number of hooked needles operated by treadles. Power was applied to knitting machines only in the 1840s, but by 1900 the industry was largely in factories. The last commercially worked hand frames finally ceased work at Calverton in 1955.*

ABOVE RIGHT: *Knitting machines in a modern factory. Production rates of five to six million stitches a minute are common. A good hand knitter can produce a hundred stitches a minute; Lee's stocking frame produced about a thousand.*

by rapiers, grippers and air and water jets. The shuttle could soon be obsolete.

KNITTING

Hosiery, a term which covers all knitted garments, is recognisable by its structure of interlocking loops. The ability of knitted fabric to stretch and mould itself to the body makes it highly popular. Leicestershire and Scotland are the main centres of the trade. Hand knitting was formerly a widespread occupation and it continued in places such as the Yorkshire Dales long after the invention of the stocking frame

by the Reverend William Lee in 1589. Framework knitting remained a domestic industry until well into the nineteenth century. The French engineer Brunel invented a circular machine in 1816 and the two methods of production are still used. Matthew Townsend's latch needle of 1849 simplified the knitting mechanism and opened the way for improvements in circular machines. Another Leicestershire inventor, William Cotton, patented the rotary knitting frame in 1864, making possible the automatic shaping of fabric to produce almost any garment. Today, com-

RIGHT AND BELOW: *For many years after their introduction into Britain in the sixteenth century, carpets were bought only by the wealthy, who often used them to cover tables or decorate walls rather than to walk on. The first carpet makers used Turkish techniques: upright looms and the Ghiordes knot which brought both ends of each tuft to the surface. Hand-knotted carpets took a long time to make, but the intricate designs that were possible ensured work for makers supplying the luxury market. The weaver in the engraving (right) is following the pattern marked out in exact detail on the card above his head. Weaving began in the seventeenth century. Demand grew slowly and carpets were not bought by the masses until the nineteenth century. The engraving of the carpet loom (below) was made in the 1840s, when Jacquard's punched cards were used to produce the patterns. The long frames held bobbins of worsted yarns, one frame per colour, which were raised into loops on a linen warp. The weaver was helped by a boy or girl known as a drawer.*

ABOVE: *An Axminster carpet being woven on a modern broadloom, one of the largest and most intricate machines in the textile industry. It weaves about eighteen rows a minute.*

BELOW: *A Harris tweed weaver and his treadle loom. He is one of the seven hundred who produce this famous cloth, ninety per cent of which is sold abroad. The survival of a cottage industry in a place so remote as the Outer Hebrides is a remarkable feature of the modern woollen industry. The islanders had long made their own cloth, but during a famine in the 1840s the Dowager Catherine Herbert, who owned the Harris estate, paid instructors to teach girls to weave more attractive designs and also found customers for their work in London. The Harris Tweed Association was founded in 1909 to see that standards are maintained.*

RIGHT: *Fulling, the thickening and cleaning of newly woven cloth, is an ancient craft, illustrated by this carving on a Roman gravestone. The fuller stands in a tub of warm soft water and tramples underfoot cloth covered with a detergent such as fuller's earth. Friction causes wet woollen fibres to mat together, or felt, reducing the size of a piece of cloth by as much as a third. Behind the fuller is a rail with a length of cloth hanging up to dry. The 'walking' of cloth continued in remote parts of the British Isles until the early twentieth century.*

BELOW: *Field names tell much about old industrial sites. A tenter field indicates that fulling was carried on nearby. Other clues are references to kilns and bracken, particularly if they occur close together or near a tenter field. From late medieval times bracken was burned to provide potash, which was used by the fuller as a detergent. Potash soap gave the cleanest wool and cloth for dyeing and its production in the Lake District enabled Kendal to become an important dyeing centre. The map shows the site of the old fulling mill at Pennington, near Ulverston. Bracken was close at hand and was burned in the kiln built downwind from the tenter fields. This grouping of fulling mill, tenter field, kiln and bracken occurs in numerous places on the western side of Britain.*

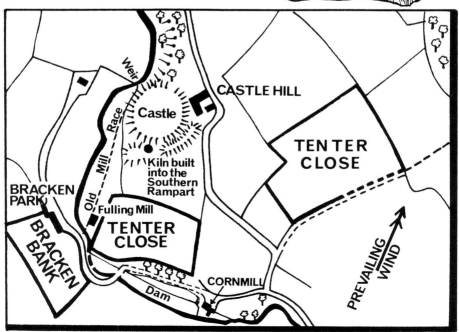

Fulling was the first woollen process to be mechanised; there are records of water-powered mills in Cumbria as early as 1135. It was only in the second half of the twentieth century that the use of hammers became obsolete. Stocks, as the machines were called, were of various sizes. Those in the photograph above were used until the late 1970s at Meadowcroft Mill, Lancashire, which specialised in heavy industrial fabrics. The 'neb' part of the feet, which turned the cloth, can be clearly seen. The engraving below shows mid nineteenth-century stocks of a much lighter construction. The tub was for preparing soapy water. The introduction of fulling mills was largely responsible for concentrating the woollen (as opposed to the worsted) industry in hilly districts. It also gave men with capital a chance to enter the industry by building mills, a development which helped to undermine the power of the town-based guilds.

puter-controlled knitting machines work at the rate of six million stitches a minute.

FINISHING

After leaving the weaver, cloth is examined and faults are mended. Then follows a series of 'wet' and 'dry' processes which stabilise the cloth so that it retains its shape and feel when it reaches the buyer. A great number of finishes are possible. Men's fine worsted suiting must have a clear smooth surface; dress fabrics, skirtings and coatings may be given a crisp or a soft feel; blankets are given a raised surface. It was once the fuller's job to thicken woollen cloth in his stocks, stretch it on tenterframes and crop the nap. These

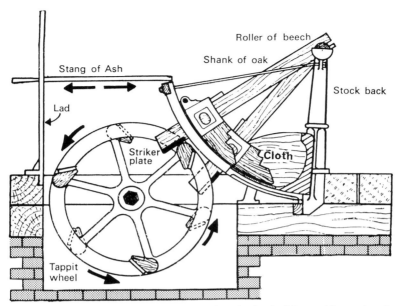

ABOVE: *How fulling stocks work. Cloth is placed in the 'box' of the machine against the curved wooden breast and is pounded by a pair of hammers which are lifted and released alternately by tappit wheels. The 'feet' of the hammers are so shaped that the cloth is constantly turned. When the machine is stopped, the hammers are held in the 'up' position by the stangs which are thrust into slots in the feet.*

BELOW: *The sign of the Pandy Inn at Tonypandy, South Wales. 'Pandy', which means fulling mill, occurs in over three hundred Welsh place names. On the right is the water-powered Tonypandy Mill, built in 1738 to process wool from the Rhondda farms.*

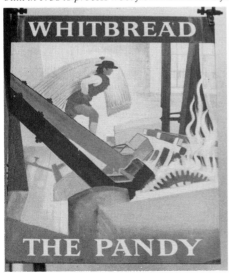

operations, which took days to complete, are now done by high-speed machinery.

DYEING

Wool may be dyed at various stages of production, but the general rule is to leave the dyeing until as late as possible. When dyed in the raw state after scouring, wool is said to be *stock dyed*. Yarn, tops and finished fabric are also dyed, *piece dyeing* being the most common. Before the nineteenth century most dyes came from plants such as woad (blue) and madder (red). The growth of scientific knowledge revolutionised the industry and a huge range of dyes and pigments is now available.

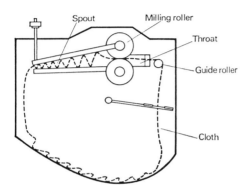

Fulling stocks have been replaced by rotary milling machines (below), in which the cloth, stitched at the ends to form an endless rope, is passed between weighted rollers. The machine was patented by John Dyer, of Trowbridge, in 1833 (see diagram left). It greatly increased production and gave more control over the shrinkage process.

RIGHT: *For hundreds of years cloth was tentered in the open air; only with the building of large mills was it possible to bring the seams indoors. This 60 yard (55 metre) seam at Higher Mill, Helmshore, Lancashire, was originally set up in a nearby field in the 1850s and because of its great length was named the 'Great Eastern' after Brunel's famous ship. It was transferred to a heated room early in the twentieth century. The photograph shows newly fulled cloth about to be fixed on the tenterhooks.*

BELOW: *A tenter seam at Otterburn Mill, Northumberland, one of the few that still dry and stretch cloth in the open air. The two rows of tenterhooks can be seen clearly.*

RIGHT: *The spiky heads of the teasel plant have long been used for scratching and softening the surface of woollen cloth. Though wire hooks have been introduced, teasels are still popular for finishing cloth and this engraving from the 1840s shows their use in machine raising. Workmen first set teasel heads in long frames called 'rods', which are fixed to the revolving cylinders of 'gig mills'. In these machines, which have changed little since their introduction in the early sixteenth century, the cloth passes in one direction and the cylinder in the other.*

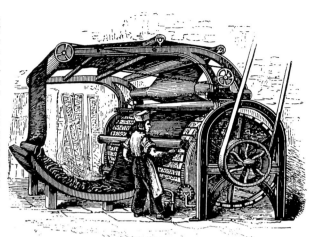

LEFT: *Hand raising of cloth in the mid nineteenth century, a process known as 'rowing'. A skilled raiser has a feel for teasels which enables him to achieve the right combination of large and small and of old and new. Some cloths are raised when wet, others when dry; the difference in the finish is considerable.*

RIGHT: *The 'broad perpetual' was one of several machines which took over the work of shearmen during the early nineteenth century. The huge hand-operated shears were replaced with a spiral cutting blade mounted on the cylinder visible at the top of the picture. One of these machines was seen in 1830 by Edwin Budding, engineer in a Stroud woollen mill. It gave him the idea 'for shearing the vegetable surface of lawns and grass' and inspired the development of the lawnmower.*

An early nineteenth-century finishing shop. At the back of the room a workman is 'rowing' cloth with a teasel bat to raise the nap. (Note the piles of teasels on the extreme left of the picture.) On the right are the shearing boards and the heavy shears with which the uneven nap was cropped to produce a smooth surface. Heart-shaped lead weights from the frame in the foreground were added to the shears to increase pressure. One workman is sprinkling water on a piece to make the shearing easier.

FELTMAKING

A small but important sector of the woollen industry is concerned with making a non-woven material known as pressed felt. By using heat, moisture, pressure and vibration, the feltmaker causes the woollen fibres to lock together to produce fabrics which range from the soft and bulky to those which are so solid that they have to be cut with a saw.

Today's felts are of two distinct kinds, known as coloured and industrial. The first is used for toys, display materials and indoor bowling greens, the second for a vast number of applications. Every major industry uses felt and many companies would be unable to carry on without it. Industrial felt is made into aero-engine washers, inking rollers, piano hammers, felt-tipped pens, polishing bobs, door seals, filters, anti-vibration pads and items for many other purposes.

Feltmaking is an ancient craft and was known before the discovery of weaving. In Britain felt hatmaking has a long history, but it was the making of cheap carpets in the nineteenth century that laid the foundation of the present industry. From Leeds the industry moved to Rossendale, where the block printers, who provided the designs, achieved superior results. Rossendale also pioneered the felt slipper, a diversification which grew into an important new industry. Felt carpets were replaced by those woven on the power loom, but by then the manufacturers were beginning to find new uses for their product. That trend still continues.

PLACES TO VISIT

MUSEUMS

Bradford Industrial Museum, Moorside Mills, Moorside Road, Bradford BD2 3HP. Telephone: 0274 631756.

Broadway Tower Country Park, Broadway, Worcestershire WR12 7LB. Telephone: 0386 852390.

Calderdale Industrial and Pre-Industrial Museum, Central Works, Halifax, West Yorkshire HX1 0QG. Telephone: 0422 358087.

Cliffe Castle Art Gallery and Museum, Spring Gardens Lane, Keighley, West Yorkshire BD20 6LH. Telephone: 0535 618230 or 618231.

Coldharbour Mill, Uffculme, Cullompton, Devon EX15 3EE. Telephone: 0884 840960.

Cotswold Woollen Weavers, Filkins, near Lechlade, Gloucestershire GL7 3RF. Telephone: 036786 491.

Helmshore Textile Museum, Holcombe Road, Helmshore, Rossendale, Lancashire BB4 4NP. Telephone: 0706 226459. Water-powered fulling mill.

Lavenham Guildhall, Market Place, Lavenham, Suffolk CO10 9QZ. Telephone: 0787 247646. (National Trust.)

Leeds Industrial Museum, Armley Mill, Canal Road, Armley, Leeds LS12 2QF. Telephone: 0532 637861.

Museum of the Welsh Woollen Industry, Dre-fach Felindre, Llandysul, Dyfed SA44 5UP. Telephone: 0559 370929.

Newtown Textile Museum, 7 Commercial Street, Newtown, Powys. Telephone: 0938 554656.

Piece Hall Pre-Industrial Museum and Art Gallery, Piece Hall, Halifax, West Yorkshire. Telephone: 0422 358087. A section of the old cloth market (well worth a visit in its own right) has been made into a textile museum.

Swansea Maritime and Industrial Museum, Museum Square, Maritime Quarter, Swansea, Glamorgan SA1 1UN. Telephone: 0792 650351.

Tolson Memorial Museum, Ravensknowle Park, Wakefield Road, Huddersfield HD5 8DJ. Telephone: 0484 530591 or 541455.

Welsh Folk Museum, St Fagans, Cardiff CF5 6SB. Telephone: 0222 569441. Includes a working woollen mill.

WOOLLEN MILLS

Mills open to visitors include:

Cambrian Woollen Mill, Llanwrtyd Wells, Powys LD5 4SD. Telephone: 05913 211.

Curlew Weavers Woollen Mill, Rhydlewis, Llandysul, Dyfed SA44 5RL. Telephone: 0239 851357.

Islay Woollen Mill, Bridgend, Isle of Islay, Argyll. Telephone: 0496 810563. This is a working mill which has a remarkably fine collection of antique machinery, including two spinning jennies and a slubbing billy.

Maesllyn Woollen Mill and Museum, Maesllyn, Llandysul, Dyfed. Telephone: 0239 851251.

Moelwyn Mill, Tanygrisiau, near Blaenau Ffestiniog, Gwynedd.

Penmachno Woollen Mill, near Betws-y-Coed, Gwynedd LL24 0PP. Telephone: 0690 710545.

Rock-Mill, Capel-Dewi, Llandysul, Dyfed SA44 4PH. Telephone: 0559 362356.

Trefriw Woollen Mills, Trefriw, near Llanrwst, Gwynedd LL27 0NQ. Telephone: 0492 640462.

Tregwynt Woollen Mill, Castlemorris, Haverfordwest, Dyfed SA62 5UX. Telephone: 03485 225.

In addition, hand spinning and weaving are demonstrated by a number of cottagers in the Outer Hebrides.